FEB 1 0 2016

ELK GROVE VILLAGE PUBLIC LIBRARY

3 1250 01127 2147

19

P9-DCQ-749

Discarded By Elk Grove
Village Public Library

Elk Grove Vlg.Public Library
1001 Wellington Avenue
Elk Grove Village, IL 60007
(847)-439-0447

For Annabelle and James

WILDLIFE RESCUE

Koala
HOSPITAL

Written and photographed
by Suzi Eszterhas

Owlkids Books

Table of Contents

A Note from Suzi

I've photographed a lot of baby animals. But koalas are probably the cutest ones I have ever seen! When I saw my first koala joey, a little female named Josie, I thought about how much she looked just like a plush toy. It was hard to imagine her surviving all alone in the forest, when she should have been in her mother's pouch. I felt so relieved that she had been rescued.

The Koala Hospital in Port Macquarie, Australia, can be a very busy place. There were lots of people zipping around the hospital caring for one koala after another, and most of these people volunteered their time just so that they could be around the koalas. Young or old, man or woman, they all had one thing in common—they just loved koalas. It was so inspiring to meet people who wanted to help animals that much!

I wish everyone loved koalas as much as the people at the Koala Hospital do. As a wildlife photographer, I've traveled the world to see and photograph a lot of different animals, and I think koalas are very special. I wrote this book because I believe we've got to convince the world that we need koalas and that their forest homes are worth protecting. So read on—I hope you'll agree.

Suzi Eszterhas

Welcome to the Koala Hospital

On the southeastern coast of Australia is a special hospital with some very cute and cuddly patients—koalas! For over 40 years, the Koala Hospital in Port Macquarie has been rescuing and treating sick and injured koalas. Each year, over 200 koalas arrive at the world's only hospital that specializes in caring for these adorable animals that live on the continent of Australia .

The town of Port Macquarie has many koalas roaming around. People who live there often see koalas feeding in the eucalyptus trees right in their backyards. But actually, it's people who are living in the koalas' backyards: Scientists have found koala fossils in Australia that are 20 million years old. That's long before people lived there!

For koalas, living with people can be challenging and dangerous. That's where the Koala Hospital comes in. A big-time koala lover, Cheyne Flanagan (right) runs the hospital with her team of volunteers. They all give their time and energy to help give koalas a second chance at life.

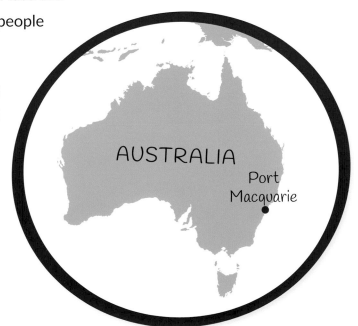

AUSTRALIA

Port Macquarie

When Koalas Get Hurt

Meet Buster. Buster is an adult male koala that came to the hospital after he was hit by a car. Busy roads with fast-moving vehicles often pass right through koala habitats. This makes for a dangerous situation for koalas, which have to cross roads every day to get from one tree to the next.

When he arrived at the hospital, Buster felt scared and hurt. Cheyne and her team immediately placed him in a laundry basket. The small space of the basket is like a nest that keeps koalas contained while making them feel safe. The hospital team must learn to "think like a koala" and mimic their slow, easy movements so they don't frighten the koala patients.

Koalas that live around houses also have to walk across people's backyards. People who have pet dogs often don't realize that their dog might chase and attack a koala. Sadly, many of the injured koalas at the hospital come in after being bitten by dogs.

 These bright-yellow signs warn people to drive slowly and carefully in koala country.

Helping Sick Koalas

Koalas that share their habitat with people are more likely to get sick than koalas in the wild. Some of these illnesses can kill a koala if left untreated.

Rescuing a sick koala can be tricky because koalas often sit high in a tree when they are not feeling well. They often stay asleep there for days at a time. The Koala Hospital's rescue team has learned how to gently coax a sick koala down from a tree. Rescuers wave a pole with a towel flag above the koala's head to encourage it to climb down. The team then rushes the koala patient to the hospital in the koala ambulance.

People who have a sick koala living in their yard can call the Koala Hospital, day or night, and the rescue team is always ready to help.

A Place to Heal

The hospital's medical team carefully examines all patients that arrive at the Koala Hospital. When frightened, a koala will lash out and use its claws for protection, and a scratch from a koala can be very painful. So before an exam, the team will wrap a koala's body in a canvas bag, keeping its sharp claws tucked away. The canvas bag keeps a koala still so that the team can safely listen to its heart and lungs, check its eyes, ears, and body temperature, and feel its body for injuries.

Caring for sick koalas takes a team of kind, gentle veterinarians and koala caretakers working around the clock.

Eye infections are common and can take weeks to treat. This koala is getting her daily light-therapy treatment, which involves some state-of-the-art equipment. The red light might look a bit scary, but she can't feel a thing. This light therapy, some strong medicine, and some tender loving care will help her eyes heal so that she can return to the wild where she belongs.

Koalas are solitary animals, so the male koalas do not stay with the mother and joey. As with many animals, the mother koalas are the sole caretakers for their babies.

Orphaned Koalas

Although koalas might look like teddy bears, they are actually not bears at all. Koalas are marsupials, like kangaroos and opossums. A marsupial female has a pouch on her belly to carry her baby. A baby koala stays safe and warm in its mother's pouch for the first six months of life. A koala baby is called a joey. It is pink, hairless, and only as big as a jelly bean when it is born. After it is born, the joey crawls up its mother's belly fur and into her pouch where it will stay hidden for months.

Sadly, baby koalas sometimes lose their mothers or become separated from them. That's when human "moms" from the Koala Hospital step in to take care of the orphaned joeys.

When a joey is six months old, it will start to emerge from its mother's pouch and see the world for the first time.

Tender Loving Care

After losing its mom, a joey feels very scared, lonely, and sad. Upon arrival at the hospital, caretakers give an orphaned joey a stuffed animal to cling to, which makes it feel safe.

The caretakers make sure they are extra gentle and quiet when examining these little ones. Joeys require special care and need to be touched, cuddled, and hugged frequently, or they could become depressed and very sick.

After a careful examination by the hospital team, a healthy joey will go to a human foster mother and live in her house full time.

Foster Mothers

Foster moms are very good at pretending to be koala mothers. In the wild, joeys stick to their mothers like glue. It's no different in foster homes! A new orphan isn't shy for long and will quickly develop a strong bond to the foster mom. The joey will cling to the foster mom as she moves around the house, even while she watches TV, washes the dishes, or reads a book. Snuggled up against its foster mom, an orphaned joey feels safe and cozy.

In the wild, koala joeys nurse every few hours and get all of the nutrients they need from their mothers' milk. Foster moms take over this job and even wake up in the middle of the night to feed the joey. They put milk in an empty syringe, which is the perfect size for the joey's tiny mouth.

Some very devoted foster moms have cared for baby koalas for over 20 years, raising dozens of joeys.

Learning to Climb

In addition to growing big and strong, an orphaned joey must learn how to climb. As an adult, a koala will have to climb trees that are over 100 feet (30.5 meters) tall, so it is very important for the joey to practice climbing every day. Here, this joey's foster mom has built him a special play tree that is the koala's own climbing gym. Towel padding helps his claws easily grip the tree, which is low to the ground in case he falls.

This joey's foster mom has also placed leaves on his play tree. At seven months old, he will start nibbling eucalyptus leaves for the first time.

Time for a Checkup

When a joey has grown big enough to weigh 5 pounds (2.3 kilograms), it's time to leave foster care and return to the Koala Hospital. It will spend time with other young koalas in an outdoor enclosure before returning to the wild. The hospital is careful to keep the young koalas separate from the adults, who can sometimes be aggressive toward the youngsters.

Back at the hospital, Cheyne is happy to see that this joey has grown to be so big and healthy. She listens to the joey's heart again, checks to make sure its coat is thick and shiny, and looks at its teeth to make sure they are ready for grinding down leaves. A healthy checkup means that the joey is ready to live outdoors.

Cheyne listens to a joey's heartbeat using a stethoscope, just like a doctor would use for a person.

A healthy baby is a growing baby, so caretakers weigh a joey weekly to make sure it is gaining enough weight.

Tagging and Tracking

Before going outside, the joey must get an ear tag. Getting an ear tag is like getting your ears pierced, so it hurts a little bit. The ear tag is important, though, because it contains an identification number that allows scientists and observers to keep track of this koala after caretakers release him into the wild. Being able to keep track of the koalas gives researchers information that will help them conserve wild koalas and their habitats.

While Cheyne adds the ear tag, the little joey sniffs its foster mother's nose to feel comfortable and safe. This nose-sniffing is exactly how a mother and joey in the wild would communicate.

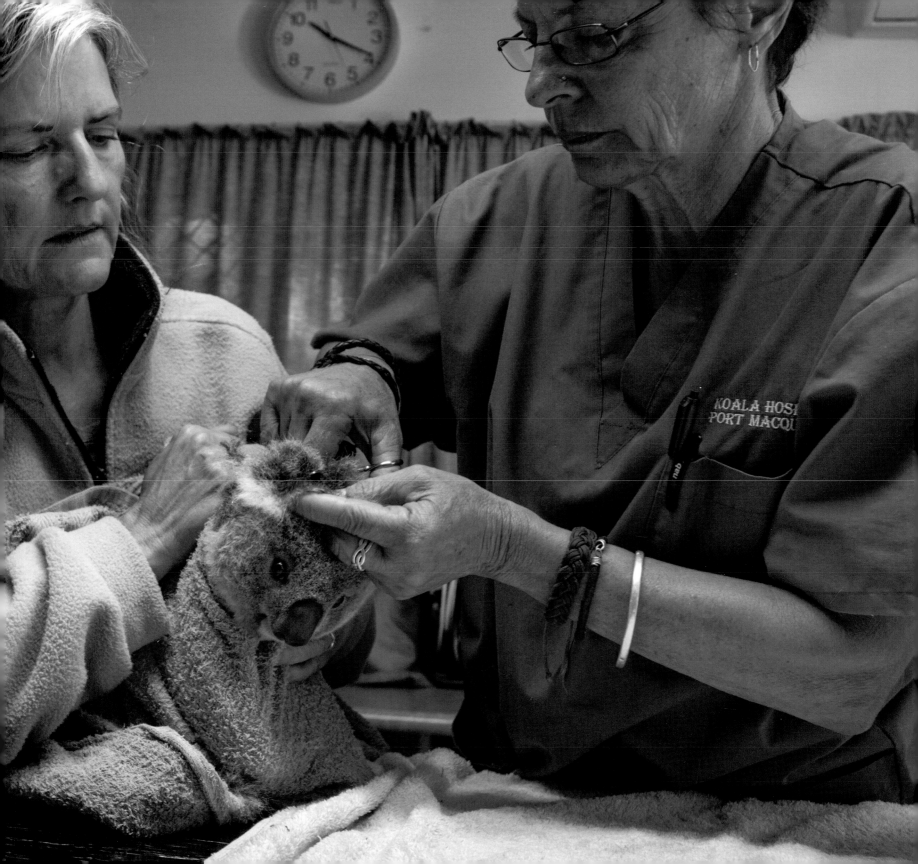

Moving Outside

Saying good-bye is not easy for a foster mother. She will miss her joey, but knows that he should live wild and free. In the Koala Hospital's outdoor juvenile yard, the joey is one step closer to freedom. He will have a chance to meet other joeys, climb real trees, breathe the forest's fresh air, and sleep under the stars. During this transition time, the hospital team leaves the young koalas alone and only enters the enclosure to feed them and clean the area. Slowly the human bond is broken, so that when the joeys are back in the wild, they stay away from people. The more they stay away from humans, cars, and houses, the safer they will be.

Getting Better

As the injured and sick patients at the hospital continue to recover, they receive 24-hour care from the team. Some koalas spend only a few days at the hospital, but others stay for weeks or even months. Taking care of koalas is a big job. Some koalas need medicine and vitamins several times a day. Some koalas even get a special milk formula to help keep their bones strong.

Though some sick koalas have to live in the indoor intensive care unit, their caretakers often bring them outside for a bit of time in nature each day. It's amazing how a little sunshine can lift a sick koala's spirits!

Leaves, Leaves, and More Leaves

Of course, the koalas at the hospital must eat. What do they eat? Leaves, leaves, and lots of leaves! A wild koala can eat up to 1 pound (0.45 kilograms) of leaves each day. To fill the koalas' hungry bellies, the hospital staff must wake up early and spend hours collecting leaves every morning.

The leaves from eucalyptus trees are a koala's favorite food. This is strange because eucalyptus leaves are poisonous to most animals. Koalas have a special digestive system that can break down the toxins in the leaves, so they can eat them all day long. Occasionally, koalas also eat flowers, buds, stems, and bark from a variety of different trees and plants, and even a little dirt. Koalas don't usually need to drink water. Their bodies are able to take in all the moisture they need from the leaves they eat.

Resting Up

Sleep is a big part of a koala's recovery at the Koala Hospital. Even healthy koalas in the wild sleep a lot. Eating leaves doesn't provide much energy, and koalas' bodies work hard at taking the toxins out of the eucalyptus leaves, so they need plenty of rest.

People used to think that eucalyptus leaves made koalas "drunk," but now scientists know that this isn't true. Koalas look sleepy and move slowly because their bodies are exhausted from working so hard to digest the leaves. Snoozing 18 hours a day makes the koala one of the greatest sleepyheads in the animal kingdom!

Koalas are mostly nocturnal. Nocturnal animals are awake at night and asleep during the day. Koalas, however, do sleep for part of the night and move around during the daytime.

A Teaching Hospital

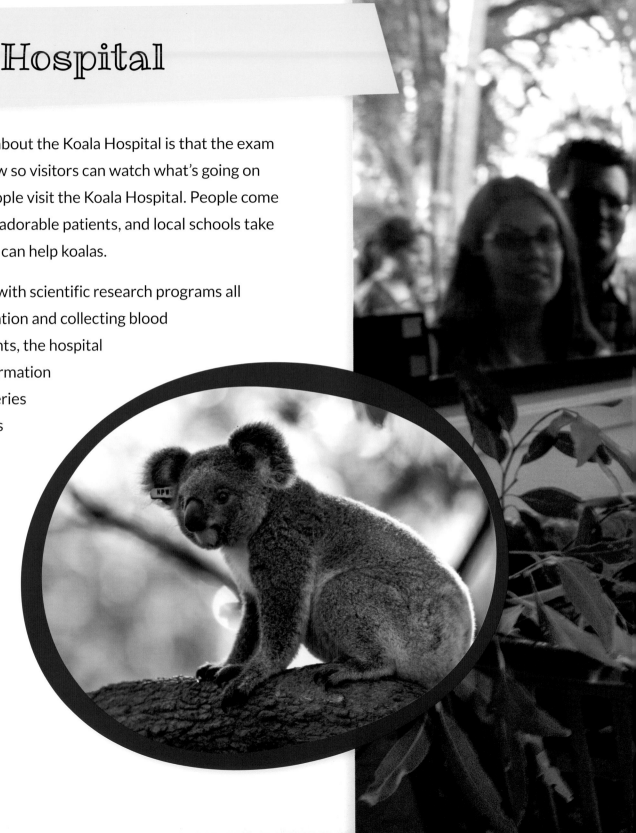

One of the wonderful things about the Koala Hospital is that the exam room has a big, open window so visitors can watch what's going on inside. Each year, over 50,000 people visit the Koala Hospital. People come from all over the world to see the adorable patients, and local schools take field trips there to learn how they can help koalas.

The Koala Hospital also partners with scientific research programs all over Australia. By sharing information and collecting blood and hair samples from their patients, the hospital supports koala research. The information helps scientists make new discoveries about koala behavior and illnesses and helps rescuers take even better care of these amazing creatures.

Back to the Wild

Most koalas at the hospital are able to return to the wild after they recover. When caretakers release them, koalas usually scamper away to freedom and climb the first tree they can find. Koalas are powerful animals with sharp, strong claws. They are able to climb even the widest eucalyptus trees quickly and easily.

Sometimes patients can't be released into the wild, such as the koala above, who is blind. Without her eyesight, she would not be able to climb or find food. She will spend the rest of her life at the hospital fulfilling the important job of koala ambassador. When people visit the Koala Hospital, she will help teach visitors about koalas and may even inspire people to help.

Conservation

Hospitals alone can't save the koala. There are only 45,000 koalas left in all of Australia. Koalas need trees and leaves to live. Every day, builders cut more and more trees down to make way for houses, farms, and roads. Without enough trees, koalas simply can't survive. About 80% of the koala's natural habitat has been destroyed.

The Koala Hospital and other people who care about koalas have started tree-planting programs throughout Australia. Students and volunteers plant seedlings for eucalyptus and other trees that provide for a good koala habitat. Unfortunately, trees grow slowly and even the best tree-planting programs can't keep up with the fast rate at which trees are being cut down.

Although laws help protect koalas themselves, they don't protect the koalas' eucalyptus-forest homes, which are being destroyed. In order to save the koala, conservation laws are needed to prevent people from destroying the koala habitat. In addition, builders and new homeowners can help keep the land koala-friendly by leaving groves of eucalyptus trees standing wherever possible.

A volunteer plants a eucalyptus tree seedling, which will grow to be a home and food for koalas.

How You Can Help Wildlife

Helping wildlife begins with you! Imagine if every person did one little thing to help animals. All those little things would add up to something very big.

- Make your yard wildlife friendly. Ask your parents if you can plant native plants, trees, and bushes in your yard. These will provide homes and food for many different types of animals, from insects to mammals. Also, consider adding ponds, birdhouses, and birdbaths to your yard.

- Tell an adult to call animal rescue if you see an animal that looks injured or sick. Whether wild or domestic, all animals need and deserve our help.

- Organize a drive to collect supplies for your local wildlife hospital. They usually need a constant supply of towels, blankets, and certain types of food. Check with your local facility to find out what their animal patients currently need.

How You Can Help Koalas

- Adopt a koala at the Koala Hospital at www.koalahospital.org.au.

- Join the Koalas for Kids Club of the Australian Koala Foundation at www.savethekoala.com.

- Organize a fundraiser at school to raise money to help save koalas. Donate the money to a koala conservation organization.

Kids Ask Suzi

1. **Have you ever held a koala?** Yes. And he was very soft and smelled really good. He smelled very much like the eucalyptus leaves he was eating.

2. **What do you think is the coolest thing about koalas?** It's hard to pick one thing—but I do love the fact that koalas have fingerprints. They are one of the few mammals (besides primates) to have them. Their fingerprints are just like human fingerprints—each one is unique.

3. **Do koalas make any noises?** Yes. In fact, the males make a "bellow," which is really loud and kind of like a koala roar. They do this to attract females. The joeys also make high-pitched yipping noises when frightened.

4. **Have you ever been scratched by a koala?** Never. The hospital is very good at keeping the koalas calm, so that they rarely get aggressive. I felt really safe while I was there. But it's important to remember that koalas are wild animals and can be dangerous if they feel threatened, so they should never be approached in the wild.

5. **How do koalas get their name?** The word "koala" comes from an old Aboriginal word meaning "no drink." Koalas rarely ever drink water because they get moisture from the leaves they eat.

6. **Have you ever seen a koala in the wild?** Yes, I have, and I love seeing them in the wild, happy in the trees where they should be. Of course, in some Australian towns you can see them in people's yards. But it's fun to explore a real eucalyptus forest and look for koalas high in the trees.

7. **Are there different kinds of koalas?** All koalas are part of the same species. But koalas in the southern parts of Australia are considerably larger and have thicker fur than those in the north. Scientists think this is an adaptation to keep them warm in the colder southern winters.

8. **I've heard people call koalas "koala bears." Are they really bears?** No. Koalas are not bears and are not related to bears at all. Their closest living relative is a wombat, which is another marsupial in Australia.

Glossary

conservation
Protecting animals, plants, and natural resources.

ear tag
An ear tag contains an identification number that allows scientists and observers to keep track of a koala after it's been released into the wild.

eucalyptus (trees and leaves)
Eucalyptus leaves are the main food koalas eat. The leaves are poisonous to most animals, but koalas have a special digestive system that allows them to eat these leaves.

foster mother
Sometimes baby koalas lose their mothers. Human mothers, called foster mothers, step in to take care of the babies.

habitat
The place where an animal naturally lives.

joey
A baby koala is called a joey.

juvenile yard
The juvenile yard is a special outdoor enclosure at the hospital just for young koalas. It keeps them safe while they get used to living outside again.

koala ambassador
If a koala cannot be released back into the wild, it becomes a koala ambassador. When people visit the hospital, the ambassador helps teach visitors about koalas. The ambassador also serves as a symbol that helps raise awareness about the importance of koala conservation.

marsupial
Koalas are part of the marsupial family. Female marsupials have pouches to carry their babies. Kangaroos and wombats are other marsupials.

nocturnal
Nocturnal animals are awake at night and asleep during the day. Koalas are mainly nocturnal, though they do move around during the daytime and sometimes sleep for part of the night.

teaching hospital
A hospital that treats patients and trains other doctors, nurses, and volunteers.

Index

Acknowledgments

Cheyne Flanagan and the entire team of staff and volunteers at the Koala Hospital in Port Macquarie, Australia; Deborah Tabart of the Australian Koala Foundation in Brisbane, Australia; Al Mucci at Dreamworld, Coomera, Australia; Lone Pine Sanctuary, Brisbane, Australia; and Currumbin Wildlife Sanctuary, Currumbin, Australia.

Sources

Australian Koala Foundation; savethekoala.com

Cheyne Flanagan (hospital supervisor at the Port Macquarie Koala Hospital), in discussion with the author, 2013.

Cox, Karin. *The Koala: A Nation's Icon*. Leichhardt, NSW, Australia: Steve Parish Publishing, 2007.

Deborah Tabart (CEO of the Australian Koala Foundation), in discussion with the author, 2013.

Flanagan, Cheyne. *Koala Rehabilitation Manual*. NSW, Australia: Koala Preservation Society of NSW, 2009.

Koala Hospital; koalahospital.org.au

Sharp, Ann. *The Koala Book*. Gretna, Louisiana: Pelican Publishing Company, 1995.

Text and photographs © 2015 Suzi Eszterhas

All rights reserved. No part of this publication may be reproduced, stored in a retrieval system, or transmitted in any form or by any means, without the prior written permission of Owlkids Books Inc., or in the case of photocopying or other reprographic copying, a license from the Canadian Copyright Licensing Agency (Access Copyright). For an Access Copyright license, visit www.accesscopyright.ca or call toll-free to 1-800-893-5777.

Owlkids Books acknowledges the financial support of the Canada Council for the Arts, the Ontario Arts Council, the Government of Canada through the Canada Book Fund (CBF) and the Government of Ontario through the Ontario Media Development Corporation's Book Initiative for our publishing activities.

Published in Canada by
Owlkids Books Inc.
10 Lower Spadina Avenue
Toronto, ON M5V 2Z2

Published in the United States by
Owlkids Books Inc.
1700 Fourth Street
Berkeley, CA 94710

Library and Archives Canada Cataloguing in Publication

Eszterhas, Suzi, author
    Koala hospital / Suzi Eszterhas.

(Wildlife rescue ; 1)
Includes bibliographical references and index.

ISBN 978-1-77147-140-4 (bound)

    1. Koala--Conservation--Australia--Juvenile literature.
2. Koala--Ecology--Australia--Juvenile literature. 3. Wildlife rescue--Australia--Juvenile literature. I. Title.

QL737.M384E89 2015   j599.2'5   C2014-908459-5

Library of Congress Control Number: 2015934533

Edited by: Jessica Burgess
Designed by: Diane Robertson
Consultants: Dr. Mark Eldridge and Dr. Adam Polkinghorne

Manufactured in Shenzhen, China, in May 2015, by C&C Joint Printing Co.
Job #201500401R1

A   B   C   D   E   F

Publisher of Chirp, chickaDEE and OWL
www.owlkidsbooks.com